Alpaca
Coloring Book
For Adults

30 Hand Drawn, Doodle and Folk Art
Paisley, Henna and Zentangle Style
Alpaca Coloring Pages

By
Louise Ford

ISBN-13: 978-1542853859
ISBN-10: 1542853850

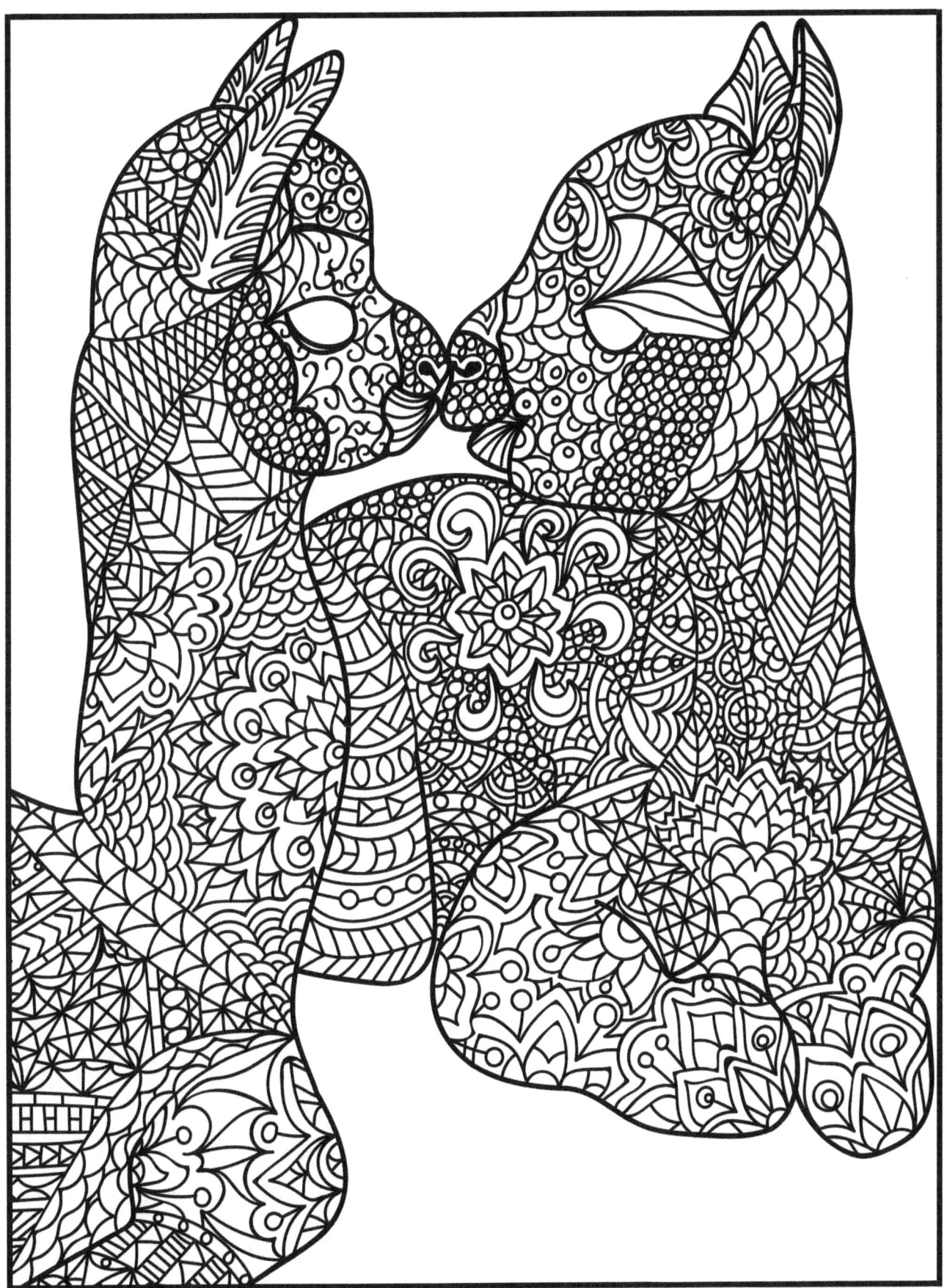

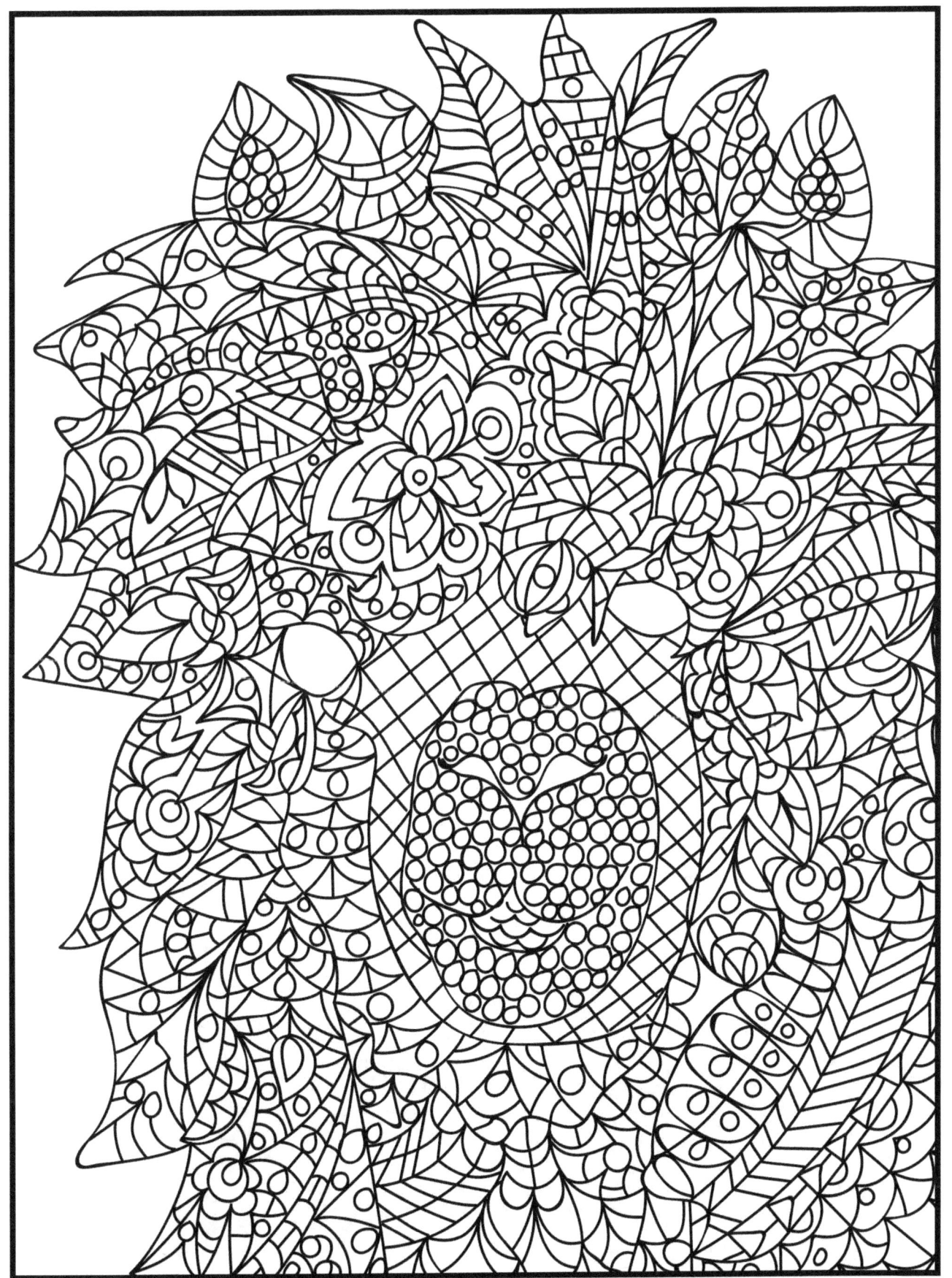

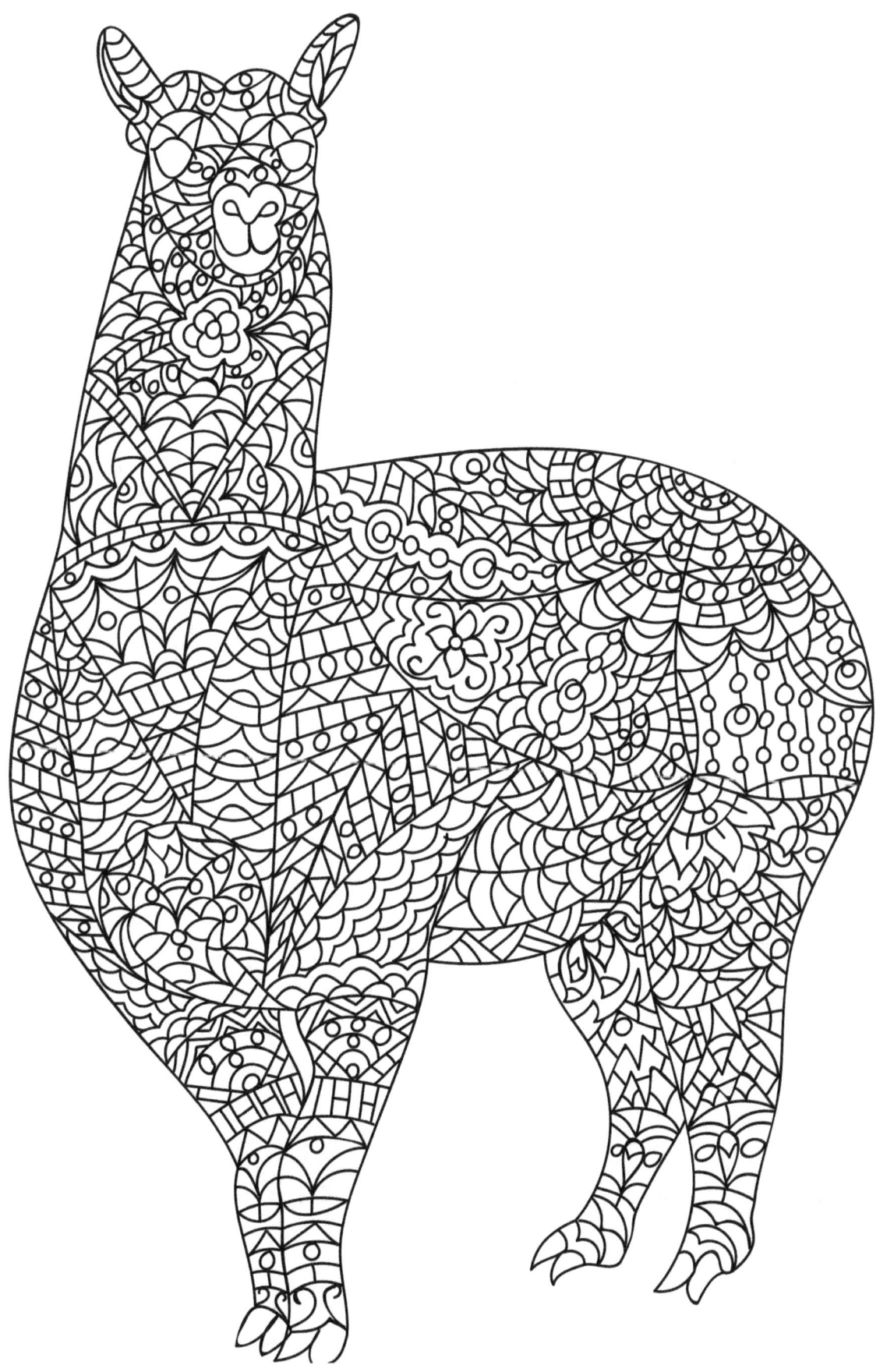

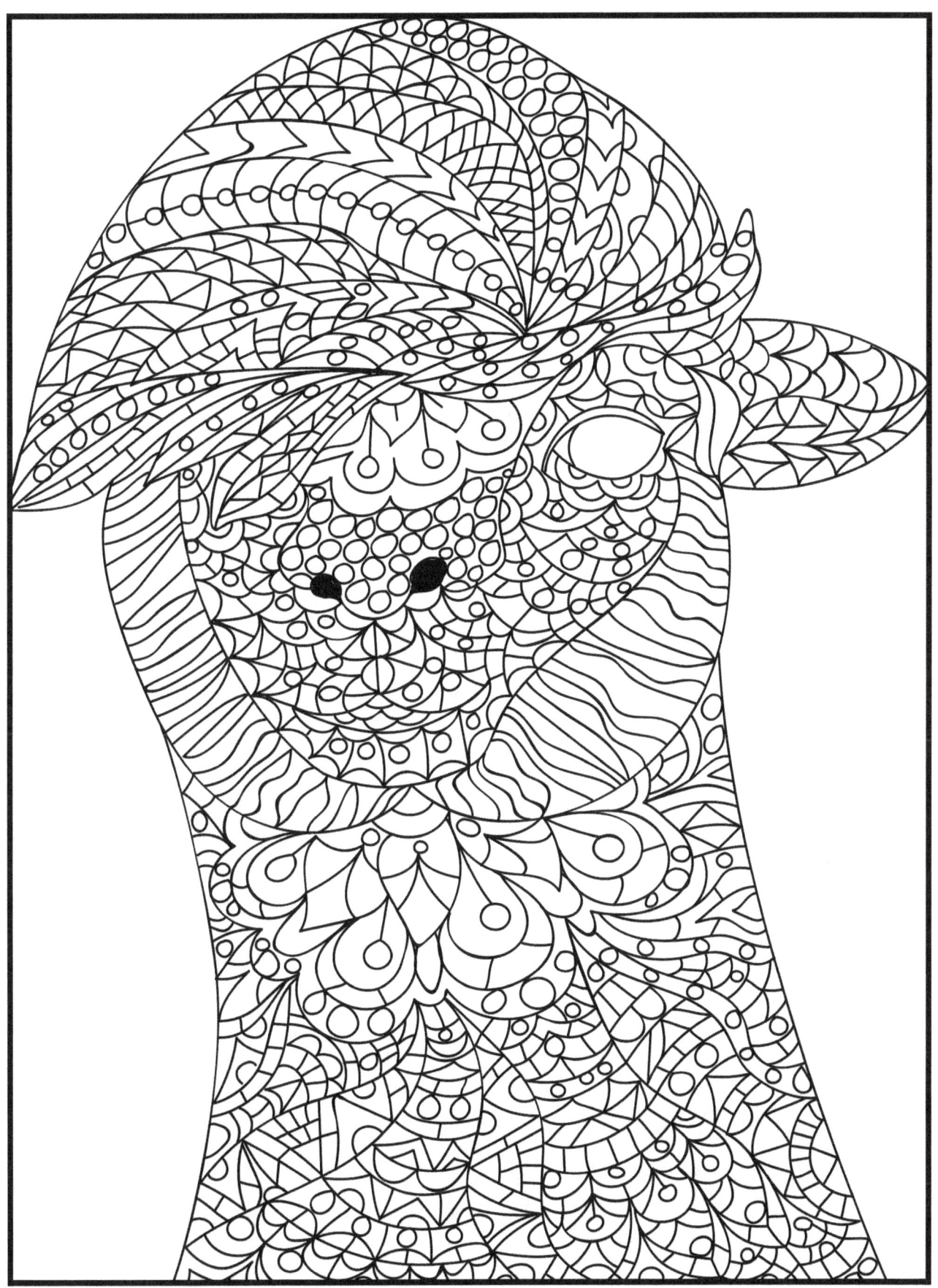

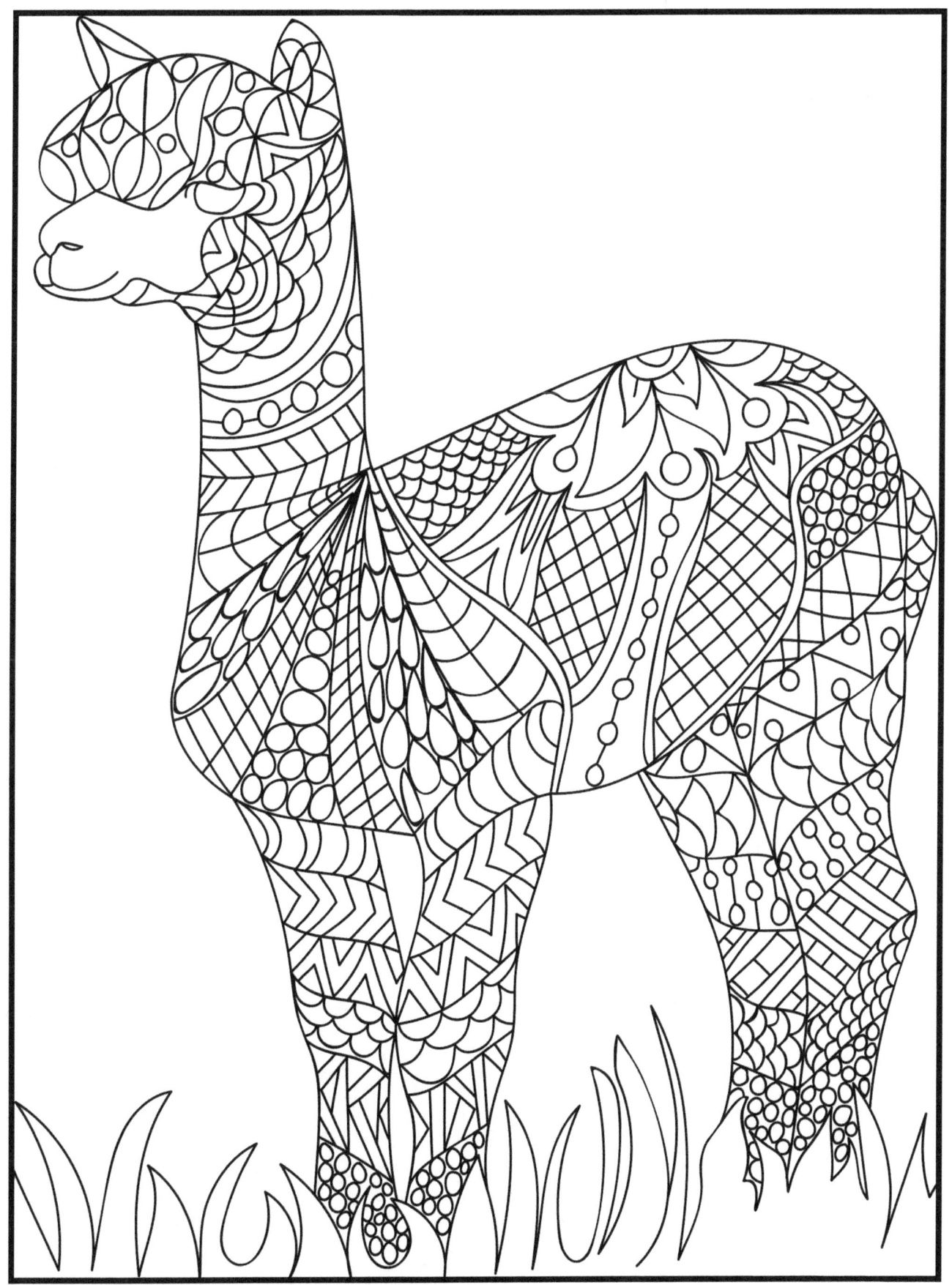

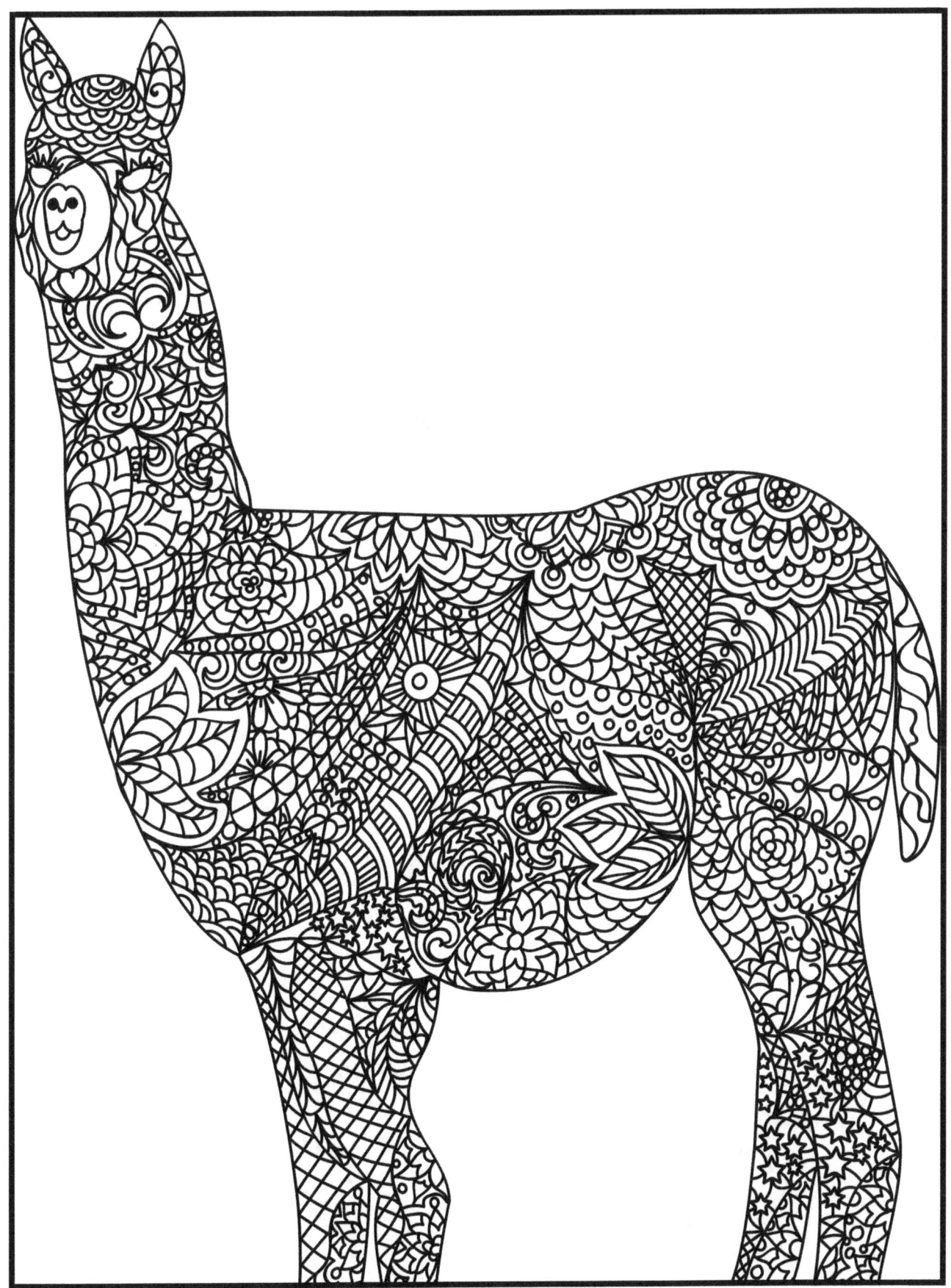

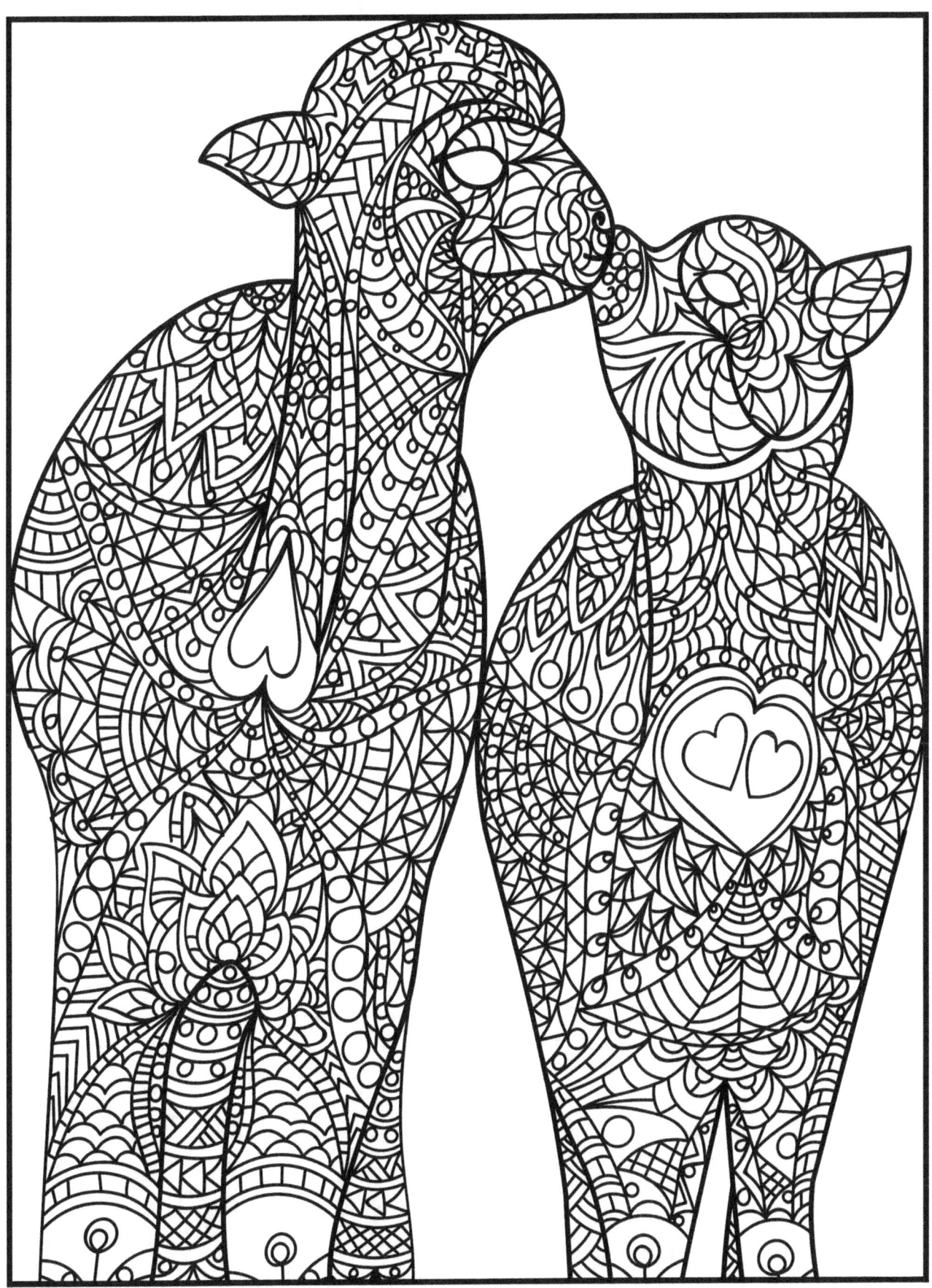

www.ingramcontent.com/pod-product-compliance
Lightning Source LLC
Chambersburg PA
CBHW081418280526
45788CB00009B/3150